In a WEEKEND
baby shower GIFTS™

The baby shower is fast approaching and you want to make something extra special for the expectant mom to open at her party. Your time is limited, but you can stitch up any of these projects in a weekend and in many cases, an evening! Designer Kristi Simpson has created 16 precious designs that will show that mom-to-be just how special she and her baby are to you. Make up a few extras while you're at it and you'll always be ready for the next baby shower.

Car Seat Carrier Cover, *page 35*

Table of Contents

On-the-Go Accessories, *page 18*

Baby's Favorites

Teddy Bear

Skill Level
 EASY

Finished Measurement
13 inches tall, standing

Materials
- Premier Yarns Home Cotton medium (worsted) weight cotton/polyester yarn (2¾ oz/ 140 yds/80g per skein):
    2 skeins #3802 cream
    1 skein each #3803 beige and #3815 sage
- Size D/3/3.25mm crochet hook or size needed to obtain gauge
- Tapestry needle
- 12mm brown animal safety eyes: 2 (see Pattern Notes)
- Fiberfill
- Stitch markers

Gauge
Head: Rnds 1–5 = 2 inches in diameter

Pattern Notes
If making Bear for child age 3 or under, embroider eyes on Bear.

Join with slip stitch as indicated unless otherwise stated.

Arms, Legs, and Head and Body are worked in continuous rounds; do not turn or join unless otherwise stated.

Mark first stitch of round and move marker as work progresses.

When changing color, drop old color until next needed. Do not fasten off unless otherwise stated.

Bear

Muzzle
Rnd 1: With cream, ch 5, sc in 2nd ch from hook, sc in each of next 2 chs, 3 sc in last ch, working across opposite side of foundation ch, sc in each of next 2 chs, 2 sc in last ch, **join** (see Pattern Notes) in first sc. (10 sc)

Rnd 2: Ch 1, sc in each of first 3 sc, 2 sc in each of next 2 sc, sc in each of next 3 sc, 2 sc in each of next 2 sc, join in first sc. (14 sc)

Rnd 3: Ch 1, sc in each of first 5 sc, 2 sc in each of next 2 sc, sc in each of next 5 sc, 2 sc in each of next 2 sc, join in first sc. (18 sc)

Rnds 4 & 5: Ch 1, sc in each sc around, join in first sc.

Leaving long end for sewing, fasten off.

With beige, using **satin stitch** (see illustration) embroider nose on Muzzle as shown in photo.

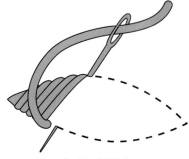

Satin Stitch

Ear
Make 2.

Rnd 1: With beige, ch 2, 4 sc in first ch, **do not join** (see Pattern Notes). **Place marker in first sc** (see Pattern Notes). (4 sc)

Rnd 2: 2 sc in each sc around. (8 sc)

Rnd 3: [Sc in next sc, 2 sc in next sc] 4 times. (12 sc)

Rnd 4: [Sc in each of next 2 sc, 2 sc in next sc] 4 times. *(16 sc)*

Rnd 5: Sc in each sc around.

Rnd 6: Sc in each sc around, join in first sc.

Leaving long end for sewing, fasten off.

Heart

With sage, ch 4, (3 tr, ch 1, 3 dc, ch 1, tr, ch 1, 3 dc, ch 1, 2 tr, ch 3, sl st) in first ch. Leaving long end for sewing, fasten off.

Arm
Make 2.

Rnd 1: With sage, ch 2, 6 sc in first ch, do not join. Place marker in first sc. *(6 sc)*

Rnd 2: 2 sc in each sc around, **changing color** *(see Stitch Guide and Pattern Notes)* to cream in last st. Fasten off sage. *(12 sc)*

Rnd 3: Working in **back lp** *(see Stitch Guide)*, sc in each sc around.

Rnd 4: Sc in each sc around, changing color to beige in last st.

Rnd 5: Sc in each sc around, changing to cream in last st.

With beige, using **straight stitch** *(see illustration)*, embroider claw on paw as shown in photo.

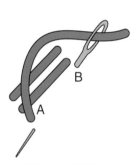

Straight Stitch

Rnd 6: With cream, sc in each sc around.

Rnd 7: Sc in each sc around, changing color to beige in last st.

Rnd 8: Sc in each sc around, changing color to cream in last st.

Rnds 9–17: Sc in each sc around. At end of last rnd, leaving long end for sewing, fasten off.

Stuff paw and lower Arm firmly with fiberfill, leaving top of Arm unstuffed to allow Arm to drape.

Leg
Make 2.

Rnd 1: With sage, ch 2, 6 sc in first ch, do not join. Place marker in first sc. *(6 sc)*

Rnd 2: 2 sc in each sc around. *(12 sc)*

Rnd 3: [Sc in next st, 2 sc in next sc] 6 times, join in first sc. Fasten off sage. *(18 sc)*

Rnd 4: Join cream in first sc, working in back lp, sc in each sc around, do not join.

Rnd 5: Sc in each sc around, changing color to beige in last st.

Rnd 6: Sc in each sc around, changing color to cream in last sc.

With beige, using straight stitch, embroider claw on paw as shown in photo.

Rnd 7: With cream, sc in each sc around.

Rnd 8: Sc in each sc around, changing color to beige in last st.

Rnds 9–11: Rep rnds 6–8.

Rnd 12: Rep rnd 6.

Rnds 13–23: [Rep rnd 7] 11 times.

Rnd 24: [Sc in next sc, **sc dec** *(see Stitch Guide)* in next 2 sc] 6 times, join in first sc. *(12 sts)*

At end of last rnd, leaving long end for sewing, fasten off.

Stuff paw and lower Leg firmly with fiberfill, leaving top of Leg unstuffed to allow Bear to sit.

Head
Rnd 1: With cream, ch 2, 6 sc in first ch, do not join. Place marker in first st. *(6 sc)*

Rnd 2: 2 sc in each sc around. *(12 sc)*

Rnd 3: [Sc in next sc, 2 sc in next sc] 6 times. *(18 sc)*

Rnd 4: [Sc in each of next 2 sc, 2 sc in next sc] 6 times. *(24 sc)*

Rnd 5: [Sc in each of next 3 sc, 2 sc in next sc] 6 times. *(30 sc)*

Rnd 6: [Sc in each of next 4 sc, 2 sc in next sc] 6 times. *(36 sc)*

Rnd 7: [Sc in each of next 5 sc, 2 sc in next sc] 6 times. *(42 sc)*

Rnd 8: [Sc in each of next 6 sc, 2 sc in next sc] 6 times. *(48 sc)*

Rnds 9–17: Sc in each sc around.

Rnd 18: [Sc in each of next 6 sc, sc dec in next 2 sc] 6 times. *(42 sts)*

Rnd 19: [Sc in each of next 5 sts, sc dec in next 2 sts] 6 times. *(36 sts)*

Rnd 20: [Sc in each of next 4 sts, sc dec in next 2 sts] 6 times. *(30 sts)*

Rnd 21: [Sc in each of next 3 sts, sc dec in next 2 sts] 6 times. *(24 sts)*

Attach eyes *(see Pattern Notes)* between rnds 12 and 13. With beige, using **backstitch** *(see illustration)*, embroider eyebrows above eyes.

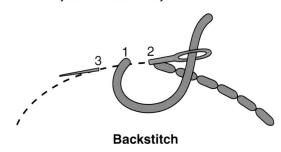

Backstitch

Align top of Muzzle with rnd 14 on Head and sew in place. Sew Ears on Head as shown in photo.

Rnd 22: [Sc in each of next 2 sts, sc dec in next 2 sts] 6 times. *(18 sts)*

Rnd 23: [Sc in next st, sc dec in next 2 sts] 6 times. *(12 sts)*

Rnd 24: 2 sc in each st around. *(24 sc)*

Stuff Head with fiberfill to desired firmness.

Body

Rnd 25: [Sc in each of next 3 sc, 2 sc in next sc] 6 times. *(30 sc)*

Rnd 26: [Sc in each of next 4 sc, 2 sc in next sc] 6 times. Place marker in rnd for Arm placement. *(36 sc)*

Rnd 27: [Sc in each of next 5 sc, 2 sc in next sc] 6 times. *(42 sc)*

Rnd 28: [Sc in each of next 6 sc, 2 sc in next sc] 6 times. *(48 sc)*

Rnds 29–36: Sc in each sc around.

With cream, sew Arms on rnd 26 of Body as shown in photo.

Align top of Heart on rnd 26 and sew in place with sage as shown in photo.

Rnds 37–44: Sc in each sc around.

Rnd 45: [Sc in each of next 6 sc, sc dec in next 2 sc] 6 times. *(42 sts)*

Rnd 46: [Sc in each of next 5 sts, sc dec in next 2 sts] 6 times. *(36 sts)*

Rnd 47: [Sc in each of next 4 sts, sc dec in next 2 sts] 6 times. *(30 sts)*

Rnd 48: [Sc in each of next 3 sts, sc dec in next 2 sts] 6 times. *(24 sts)*

Stuff Body with fiberfill to desired firmness.

Rnd 49: [Sc dec in next 2 sts] 12 times. *(12 sts)*

Rnd 50: [Sc dec in next 2 sts] 6 times. *(6 sts)*

Leaving long end for sewing, fasten off. Weave end through sts on last rnd and pull to close.

Sew Legs on bottom of Body as shown in photo. ●

Washcloth

Skill Level

■■□□ EASY

Finished Measurements

7 inches wide x 6 inches long

Materials

- Premier Yarns Home Cotton medium (worsted) weight cotton/polyester yarn (2¾ oz/ 140 yds/80g per skein):
  1 skein #3815 sage
- Size G/6/4mm crochet hook or size needed to obtain gauge
- Tapestry needle

Gauge

15 dc = 4 inches; 9 rows = 4 inches

Pattern Notes

Refer to Stitch Diagram as needed.

Chain-3 at beginning of row counts as first double crochet unless otherwise stated.

Washcloth

Row 1: Ch 28, dc in 4th ch from hook and in each rem ch across, turn. *(26 dc)*

Row 2: Ch 3 *(see Pattern Notes),* *dc in each of next 2 dc, dc around both posts of last 2 dc made, sk next st, rep from * across to last st, dc in top of beg ch-3, turn.

Rows 3–11: Ch 3, dc in each of next 2 sts, dc around both posts of last 2 dc made, dc in each of next 20 sts, dc around both posts of the last 2 dc made, sk next st, dc in top of beg ch-3, turn.

Row 12: Rep row 2.

Row 13: Ch 3, dc in each st across.

Fasten off. ●

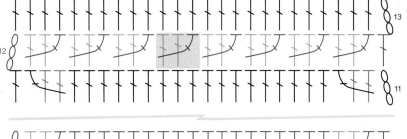
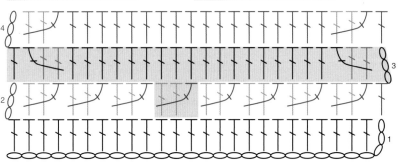

Washcloth
Stitch Diagram
***Note:** Reps shown in gray.*

STITCH KEY

○ Chain (ch)

┬ Double crochet (dc)

Diaper Cover & Headband Set

Skill Level
 ■■□□ EASY

Finished Size
0–3 months

Finished Measurements
Diaper Cover: 11 inches in waist circumference x 5 inches long

Headband: 11 inches long

Large Flower: 4½ inches in diameter

Small Flower: 3½ inches in diameter

Materials

- Premier Yarns Deborah Norville Everyday Soft Worsted medium (worsted) weight acrylic yarn (4 oz/203 yds/113g per skein):
  1 skein each #1002 cream, #1026 grenadine and #1015 sagebrush
- Size F/5/3.75mm crochet hook or size needed to obtain gauge
- Tapestry needle
- ¾-inch button: 1
- ⅝-inch button: 1
- Stitch markers

Gauge
17 sc = 4 inches; 20 rows = 4 inches

Take time to check gauge.

Pattern Notes
Refer to Stitch Diagrams as needed.

Chain-4 at beginning of round counts as first double crochet and chain-1 unless otherwise stated.

Join with slip stitch as indicated unless otherwise stated.

Diaper Cover
Row 1: With cream, ch 23, sc in 2nd ch from hook and in each rem ch across, turn. *(22 sc)*

Rows 2–14: Ch 1, sc in each sc across, turn.

Row 15: Ch 1, sc in first sc, **sc dec** *(see Stitch Guide)* in next 2 sc, sc in each of next 16 sc, sc dec in next 2 sc, sc in last sc, turn. Place marker in first and last sc. *(20 sts)*

Row 16: Ch 1, sc in first st, sc dec in next 2 sts, sc in each of next 14 sts, sc dec in next 2 sts, sc in last st, turn. *(18 sts)*

Row 17: Ch 1, sc in first st, sc dec in next 2 sts, sc in each of next 12 sts, sc dec in next 2 sts, sc in last st, turn. *(16 sts)*

Row 18: Ch 1, sc in first st, sc dec in next 2 sts, sc in each of next 10 sts, sc dec in next 2 sts, sc in last st, turn. *(14 sts)*

Row 19: Ch 1, sc in first st, sc dec in next 2 sts, sc in each of next 8 sts, sc dec in next 2 sts, sc in last st, turn. *(12 sts)*

Rows 20–31: Ch 1, sc in each st across, turn.

Row 32: Ch 1, sc in first sc, 2 sc in next sc, sc in each of next 8 sc, 2 sc in next sc, sc in last sc, turn. *(14 sc)*

Row 33: Ch 1, sc in first sc, 2 sc in next sc, sc in each of next 10 sc, 2 sc in next sc, sc in last sc, turn. *(16 sc)*

Row 34: Ch 1, sc in first sc, 2 sc next sc, sc in each of next 12 sc, 2 sc in next sc, sc in last sc, turn. *(18 sc)*

Row 35: Ch 1, sc in first sc, 2 sc in next sc, sc in each of next 14 sc, 2 sc in next sc, sc in last sc, turn. *(20 sc)*

Row 36: Ch 1, sc in first sc, 2 sc in next sc, sc in each of next 16 sc, 2 sc in next sc, sc in last sc, turn. *(22 sc)*

Rows 37–50: Ch 1, sc in each sc across, turn.

At end of last row, fasten off.

Fold Diaper Cover in half, aligning sts of first and last rows. With tapestry needle, sew side seam from top down to marker on row 15. Rep for opposite side.

Large Flower
Rnd 1: With grenadine, ch 5, sl st in first ch to form ring, **ch 4** *(see Pattern Notes)*, [(dc, ch 1) in ring] 7 times, **join** *(see Pattern Notes)* in 3rd ch of beg ch-4. *(8 dc, 8 ch-1 sps)*

Rnd 2: (Sl st, ch 1, 2 dc, ch 1, sl st) in each ch-1 sp around, join in first sl st. *(8 petals)*

Rnd 3: *Ch 2, sl st in sp between next 2 petals, rep from * around. *(8 ch-2 sps)*

Rnd 4: (Sl st, ch 1, 3 dc, ch 1, sl st) in each ch-2 sp around, join in first sl st.

Rnd 5: *Ch 3, sl st in sp between next 2 petals, rep from * around. Fasten off grenadine.

Rnd 6: Join sagebrush in any ch-3 sp, (sl st, ch 1, dc, 2 tr, ch 3, 2 tr, dc, ch 1, sl st) in same ch-3 sp, (sl st, ch 1, dc, 2 tr, ch 3, 2 tr, dc, ch 1, sl st) in each rem ch-3 sp around, join in first sl st. Fasten off.

Sew Large Flower on Diaper Cover as shown in photo.

Headband
Row 1: With cream, ch 38, dc in 4th ch from hook and in each rem ch across. Fasten off. *(36 dc)*

Row 2: Join grenadine in last st, loosely sl st in each st across. Fasten off.

Small Flower
Rnd 1: With grenadine, ch 5, sl st in first ch to form ring, ch 4, [(dc, ch 1) in ring] 5 times, join in 3rd ch of beg ch-4. *(6 dc, 6 ch-1 sps)*

Rnd 2: (Sl st, ch 1, dc, ch 1, sl st) in each ch-1 sp around, join in first sl st. *(6 petals)*

Rnd 3: *Ch 2, sl st in sp between next 2 petals, rep from * around. *(6 ch-2 sps)*

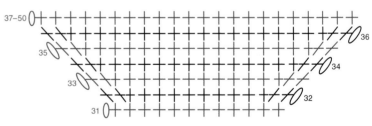

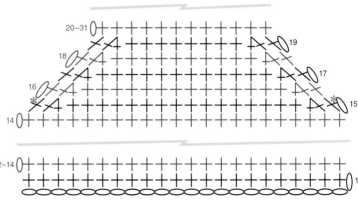

Diaper Cover & Headband Set
Diaper Cover Stitch Diagram

Rnd 4: (Sl st, ch 1, 2 dc, ch 1, sl st) in each ch-2 sp around, join in first sl st.

Rnd 5: *Ch 3, sl st in sp between next 2 petals, rep from * around. Fasten off grenadine. *(6 ch-3 sps)*

Rnd 6: Join sagebrush in any ch-3 sp, (sl st, ch 1, dc, 2 tr, ch 3, 2 tr, dc, ch 1, sl st) in same ch-3 sp, (sl st, ch 1, dc, 2 tr, ch 3, 2 tr, dc, ch 1, sl st) in each rem ch-3 sp around, join in first sl st. Fasten off.

With sewing needle and thread, sew ¾-inch button on end of Headband and ⅝-inch button on 18th and 19th sts from opposite end of Headband. Slip Small Flower over ⅝-inch button to finish. ●

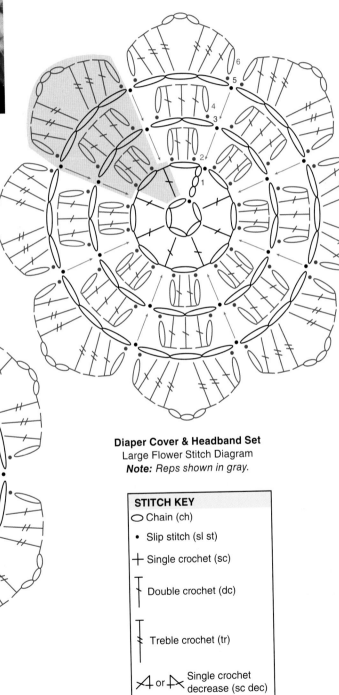

Diaper Cover & Headband Set
Large Flower Stitch Diagram
Note: Reps shown in gray.

Diaper Cover & Headband Set
Small Flower Stitch Diagram
Note: Reps shown in gray.

STITCH KEY	
◯	Chain (ch)
•	Slip stitch (sl st)
+	Single crochet (sc)
⊤	Double crochet (dc)
⊥	Treble crochet (tr)
⋌ or ⋏	Single crochet decrease (sc dec)
*	Marker

Summer Accessories

Sandals

Skill Level
 ■□□□ **EASY**

Finished Size
0–3 months

Finished Measurement
3 inches long

Materials

- Cascade Yarns Cherub Aran medium (worsted) weight nylon/acrylic yarn (3½ oz/240 yds/100g per skein):
    - 1 skein each #04 baby pink and #05 baby mint
- Size F/5/3.75mm crochet hook or size needed to obtain gauge
- Tapestry needle
- ⅜-inch button: 2
- Sewing needle and matching thread

Gauge
Sole: Rnds 1–3 = 3 inches

Pattern Notes
Refer to Stitch Diagrams as needed.

Join with slip stitch as indicated unless otherwise stated.

Left Sandal

Sole
Make 2.

Rnd 1: With pink, ch 8, sc in 2nd ch from hook, sc in each of next 3 chs, hdc in each of next 2 chs, 4 dc in last ch *(toe made)*, working across opposite side of foundation ch, hdc in each of next 2 chs, sc in each of next 4 chs, **join** *(see Pattern Notes)* in first sc. *(16 sts)*

Rnd 2: Ch 1, 2 sc in first st, sc in each of next 3 sts, hdc in next st, dc in next st, 2 dc in each of next 4 sts, dc in next st, hdc in next st, sc in each of next 3 sts, 2 sc in last st, join in first st. *(22 sts)*

Rnd 3: Ch 1, sc in first st, 2 sc in next st, sc in each of next 5 sts, [sc in next st, 2 sc in next st] 4 times, sc in each of next 5 sts, 2 sc in next st, sc in last st, join in first st. Fasten off. *(28 sts)*

Holding 2 Soles with WS tog and working through both thicknesses, join mint in first st, sl st in each st around. Fasten off.

Heel
Row 1: Beg at center back of Sole, with RS facing, sk 6 sts to right of center, join pink in 7th st, ch 1, sc in same st, sc in each of next 13 sts, turn, leaving rem sts unworked. *(14 sc)*

Rows 2 & 3: Ch 1, sc in each st across, turn.

Row 4: Ch 1, sc in each st across, ch 15 *(strap made)*, turn. *(25 sts)*

Row 5: Sc in 5th ch from hook *(sk chs count as button lp)* and in each rem ch and sc across. Fasten off.

Trim
Working in **front lp** *(see Stitch Guide)*, join mint in 3rd st on row 5 of Heel, ch 1, sl st in each st across. Fasten off.

With sewing needle and matching thread, sew button on row 5 of Heel opposite strap as shown in photo.

Toe Strap

Row 1: With pink, ch 10, sc in 2nd ch from hook and in each rem ch across. Leaving long end for sewing, fasten off

Sew Toe Strap across toe of Sandal, leaving 2 sts unworked between Toe Strap and Heel.

Flower

Rnd 1: With mint, ch 2, 5 sc in first ch, join in first sc.

Rnd 2: (Ch 1, dc, ch 1, sl st) in first sc, (sl st, ch 1, dc, ch 1, sl st) in each rem st around, join in first st.

Leaving long end for sewing, fasten off.

Right Sandal

Sole
Make 2.

Work as for Sole on Left Sandal.

Heel

Row 1: Beg at center back of Sole, sk 6 sts to left of center, join in 7th st, ch 1, sc in same st, sc in each of next 13 sts, turn, leaving rem sts unworked. *(14 sc)*

Rows 2–5: Rep rows 2–5 for Heel on Left Sandal.

Fasten off.

Trim
Work as for Trim on Heel on Left Sandal.

Toe Strap
Work as for Toe Strap on Left Sandal.

Flower
Work as for Flower on Left Sandal. ●

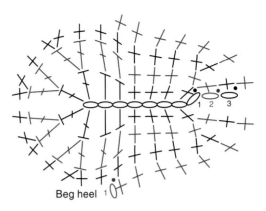

Sandals
Sole Stitch Diagram

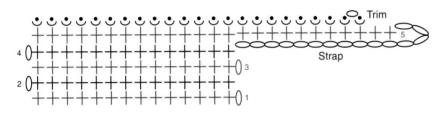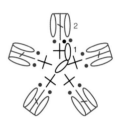

Sandals
Heel Stitch Diagram

Sandals
Flower Stitch Diagram

STITCH KEY	
◯	Chain (ch)
•	Slip stitch (sl st)
+	Single crochet (sc)
T	Half double crochet (hdc)
╫	Double crochet (dc)
⌣	Worked in front lp only

Bonnet

Skill Level

 EASY

Finished Measurements

5 inches wide x 5 inches tall

Materials

- Cascade Yarns Cherub Aran medium (worsted) weight nylon/acrylic yarn (3½ oz/240 yds/100g per skein):
  1 skein each #04 baby pink and #05 baby mint
- Size F/5/3.75mm crochet hook or size needed to obtain gauge
- Tapestry needle

Gauge

Rnds 1–5 = 2¾ inches in diameter

Pattern Notes

Refer to Stitch Diagrams as needed.

Join with slip stitch as indicated unless otherwise stated.

Chain-5 at beginning of row counts as first double crochet and chain-2 unless otherwise stated.

Special Stitch

Shell: 6 dc as indicated in instructions.

Bonnet

Rnd 1: With pink, ch 2, 10 hdc in first ch, **join** (see Pattern Notes) in first hdc. (10 hdc)

Rnd 2: Ch 1, 2 hdc in each hdc around, join in first hdc. (20 hdc)

Rnd 3: Ch 1, hdc in first hdc, 2 hdc in next hdc, [hdc in next hdc, 2 hdc in next hdc] 9 times, join in first hdc. (30 hdc)

Rnd 4: Ch 1, hdc in each of first 2 hdc, 2 hdc in next hdc, [hdc in each of next 2 hdc, 2 hdc in next hdc] 9 times, join in first hdc. (40 hdc)

Rnd 5: Ch 1, hdc in each of first 7 hdc, 2 hdc in next hdc, [hdc in each of next 3 hdc, 2 hdc in next hdc] 8 times, join in first hdc. (49 hdc)

Row 6: Now working in rows, ch 1, sc in first st, sk next 2 sts, **shell** (see Special Stitch) in next st, sk next 2 sts, *sc in each of next 2 sts, sk next 2 sts, shell in next st, sk next 2 sts, rep from * across to last st, sc in last st, turn. (7 shells)

Row 7: Ch 5 (see Pattern Notes), sk 2 next 2 dc, sc in each of next 2 dc, ch 2, sk next 2 dc, [dc in each of next 2 sc, ch 2, sk next 2 dc, sc in each of next 2 dc, ch 2, sk next 2 dc] 6 times, dc in last sc, turn.

Row 8: Ch 5, **dc dec** (see Stitch Guide) in next 2 sc, ch 2, [dc in each of next 2 dc, ch 2, dc dec in next 2 sc, ch 2] 6 times, dc in 3rd ch of beg ch-5, turn.

Row 9: Ch 1, sc in first st, 2 sc in next ch-2 sp, sc in next st, 2 sc in next ch-2 sp, [sc in each of next 2 dc, 2 sc in next ch-2 sp, sc in next st, 2 sc in next ch-2 sp] 6 times, sc in 3rd ch of beg ch-5, turn.

Rows 10–13: Rep rows 6–9.

Row 14: Rep row 6.

Row 15: Rep row 7.

Row 16: Rep row 8, **changing color** (see Stitch Guide) to mint in last st, turn.

Row 17: With mint, rep row 9, changing color to pink in last st.

Row 18: With pink, rep row 6. Fasten off.

Ties

With mint, ch 50, join in first st on row 17 of Bonnet. Rep on opposite side.

Flower

Row 1: With mint, ch 35, sl st in 4th ch from hook, *ch 3, sl st in next ch, rep from * across. Leaving long end for sewing, fasten off.

Roll piece into small rosette and secure with yarn end. Sew on Bonnet as shown in photo. ●

Bonnet
Reduced Sample of Flower
Stitch Diagram
Note: Rep shown in gray.

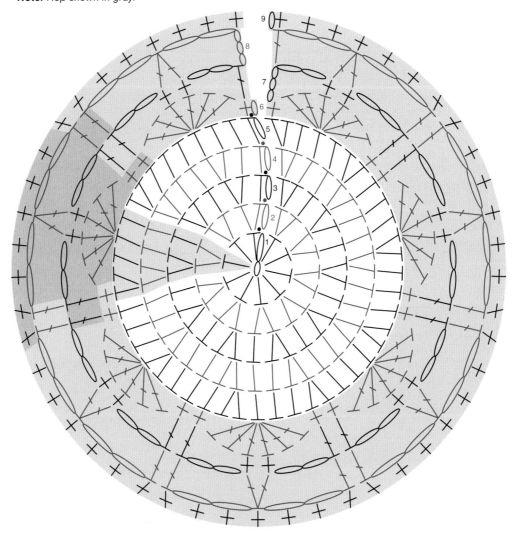

Bonnet
Stitch Diagram
Note: Reps shown in gray.

Quick & Easy Cuties

Headband

Skill Level
 EASY

Finished Measurements
1 inch wide x 10 inches in circumference

Gauge
20 hdc = 4 inches; 13 rows = 4 inches

Materials

- Caron Simply Soft Light light (DK) weight acrylic yarn (3 oz/ 330 yds/85g per skein):
    - 1 skein each #0007 capri and #0002 heavy cream
- Size F/5/3.75mm crochet hook or size needed to obtain gauge
- Tapestry needle
- Sewing needle and matching thread
- ⅝-inch button

Pattern Note
Refer to Stitch Diagrams as needed.

Headband
Row 1: With capri, ch 6, sc in 2nd ch from hook and in each rem ch across, turn. *(5 sc)*

Rows 2–36: Ch 1, working in **back lp** *(see Stitch Guide)*, hdc in each st across, turn.

Leaving long end for sewing, fasten off. Holding first and last rows tog, working through both thicknesses, sew ends tog.

Flower

Front
Row 1: With cream, ch 4, sl st in first ch to form ring, ch 1, 6 sc in ring, turn. *(6 sc)*

Row 2: Ch 1, 2 sc in each sc across, turn. *(12 sc)*

Row 3: (Sl st, ch 1, 2 dc, ch 1, sl st) in first sc, [sk next st, (sl st, ch 1, 2 dc, ch 1, sl st) in next st] 5 times, sl st in last st. Fasten off. *(6 petals)*

Back
Row 1: With cream, ch 4, sl st in first ch to form ring, ch 1, 6 sc in ring, turn. *(6 sc)*

Row 2: Ch 1, 2 sc in each sc across, turn. *(12 sc)*

Row 3: Ch 1, sc in first sc, 2 sc in next sc, [sc in next sc, 2 sc in next sc] 5 times, turn. *(18 sc)*

Row 4: (Sl st, ch 1, 2 dc, ch 1, sl st) in first sc, sk next sc, [(sl st, ch 1, 2 dc, ch 1, sl st) in next sc, sk next st] 8 times, sl st in last st. Fasten off. *(9 petals)*

Holding Front on top of Back, position Flower on Headband as shown in photo and sew in place.

With sewing needle and thread, sew button on center of Flower. ●

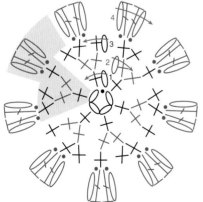

Headband
Flower Back Stitch Diagram
Note: Reps shown in gray.

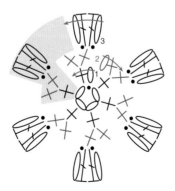

Headband
Flower Front Stitch Diagram
Note: Reps shown in gray.

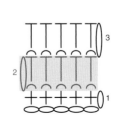

Headband
Stitch Diagram
Note: Rep shown in gray.

STITCH KEY
⬭ Chain (ch)
• Slip stitch (sl st)
✛ Single crochet (sc)
ⵜ Half double crochet (hdc)
ⵜ Double crochet (dc)
⌒ Work in back lp only
⇄ Direction of work

Burp Cloth

Skill Level
 EASY

Finished Measurements
8 inches wide x 13½ inches long

Materials

- Caron Simply Soft Light light (DK) weight acrylic yarn (3 oz/ 330 yds/85g per skein):
  1 skein #0007 capri
- Size F/5/3.75mm crochet hook or size needed to obtain gauge
- Tapestry needle

Gauge
20 hdc = 4 inches; 13 rows = 4 inches

Pattern Notes
Refer to Stitch Diagram as needed.

Chain-2 at beginning of row does not count as stitch unless otherwise stated.

Chain-3 at beginning of row counts as first double crochet unless otherwise stated.

Cloth
Row 1 (RS): Ch 36, hdc in 3rd ch from hook and in each rem st across, turn. *(34 hdc)*

Rows 2 & 3: Ch 2 *(see Pattern Notes)*, hdc in each st across, turn.

Row 4: Ch 3 *(see Pattern Notes)*, *sk next st, tr in next st, working in front of tr just made, tr in sk st, rep from * across to last st, dc in last st, turn. *(2 dc, 32 tr)*

Row 5: Rep row 2.

Row 6: Rep row 4.

Rows 7–37: [Rep row 2] 31 times.

Rows 38–40: Rep rows 4–6.

Rows 41–43: [Rep row 2] 3 times. Fasten off. ●

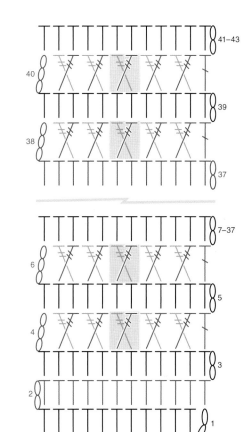

Burp Cloth
Reduced Sample of Stitch Diagram
Note: Reps shown in gray.

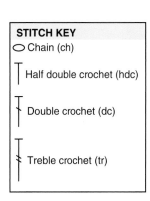

STITCH KEY
◯ Chain (ch)

T Half double crochet (hdc)

Double crochet (dc)

Treble crochet (tr)

On-the-Go Accessories

Bib

Skill Level
 ■■□□ EASY

Finished Measurements
6 inches wide x 6 inches long, excluding straps

Materials
- Premier Yarns Home Cotton medium (worsted) weight cotton/polyester yarn (2¾ oz/ 140 yds/80g per skein):
  1 skein each #3801 white, #3809 fuchsia and #3817 passionfruit
  Small amount variety of colors for sprinkles
- Size F/5/3.75mm crochet hook or size needed to obtain gauge
- Tapestry needle
- Stitch markers
- Sewing needle and matching thread
- ¾-inch button: 2

Gauge
16 sc = 4 inches; 18 rows = 4 inches

Pattern Notes
Refer to Stitch Diagrams as needed.

Join with slip stitch as indicated unless otherwise stated.

Cherry is worked in continuous rounds; do not join or turn unless otherwise stated.

Place stitch marker to mark beginning of rounds.

Special Stitch
Shell: (Sc, dc, sc) as indicated in instructions.

Bib

Base
Row 1: With passionfruit, ch 16, sc in 2nd ch from hook and in each rem ch across, turn. *(15 sc)*

Rows 2 & 3: Ch 1, sc in each sc across, turn.

Row 4: Ch 1, sc in first sc, 2 sc in next sc, sc in each of next 11 sc, 2 sc in next sc, sc in last sc, turn. *(17 sc)*

Row 5: Ch 1, sc in first sc, 2 sc in next sc, sc in each of next 13 sc, 2 sc in next sc, sc in last sc, turn. *(19 sc)*

Row 6: Ch 1, sc in first sc, 2 sc in next sc, sc in each of next 15 sc, 2 sc in next sc, sc in last sc, turn. *(21 sc)*

Rows 7–11: Ch 1, sc in each sc across, turn.

At end of last row, fasten off.

Top
Row 1: With white, ch 21, sc in 2nd ch from hook and in each rem ch across, turn. *(20 sc)*

Row 2: Ch 1, sc in each sc across, turn.

Row 3: Ch 1, sc in first sc, 2 sc in next sc, sc in each of next 16 sc, 2 sc in next sc, sc in last sc, turn. *(22 sc)*

Row 4: Ch 1, sc in first sc, 2 sc in next sc, sc in each of next 18 sc, 2 sc in next sc, sc in last sc, turn. *(24 sc)*

Rows 5 & 6: Ch 1, sc in each sc across, turn.

Row 7: Ch 1, sc in first sc, **sc dec** *(see Stitch Guide)* in next 2 sc, sc in each of next 18 sc, sc dec in next 2 sc, sc in last sc, turn. *(22 sts)*

Row 8: Ch 1, sc in first st, sc dec in next 2 sts, sc in each of next 16 sts, sc dec in next 2 sts, sc in last st, turn. *(20 sts)*

Row 9: Ch 1, sc in first st, sc dec in next 2 sts, sc in each of next 14 sts, sc dec in next 2 sts, sc in last st, turn. *(18 sts)*

Row 10: Ch 1, sc in first st, sc dec in next 2 sts, sc in each of next 12 sts, sc dec in next 2 sts, sc in last st, turn. *(16 sts)*

Row 11: Ch 1, sc in first st, sc dec in next 2 sts, sc in each of next 10 sts, sc dec in next 2 sts, sc in last st, turn. *(14 sts)*

Row 12: Sc dec in first 2 sts, sc in each of next 10 sts, sc dec in last 2 sts, turn. *(12 sts)*

Row 13: Ch 1, sc in each st across, turn.

Trim

Rnd 1: Ch 1, working in sts and row ends around Top, sc in each st and row end around, **join** *(see Pattern Notes)* in first sc.

Rnd 2: Ch 1, **shell** *(see Special Stitch)* in first sc, sl st in next sc, [shell in next sc, sl st in next sc] 8 times, place marker in last sl st made, [shell in next sc, sl st in next sc] 19 times, place marker in last sl st made, [shell in next sc, sl st in next sc] twice, join in first sc. Fasten off.

Cherry

Rnd 1: With fuchsia, ch 2, 6 sc in first ch, **do not join, place marker** *(see Pattern Notes)*. *(6 sc)*

Rnd 2: 2 sc in each sc around. *(12 sc)*

Rnd 3 (stem): (Sl st, ch 3, sc in 2nd ch from hook, sl st) in first sc. Fasten off, leaving rem sts unworked.

Finishing

Assembly

With tapestry needle and white, sew Top on last row of Base and Cherry on Top as shown in photo. With scrap yarn, sew sprinkles on Top as shown in photo.

Buttonhole Strap

Row 1: Join passionfruit in **back bar of sc** *(see illustration)* on rnd 1 of Top Trim below marker, ch 1, sc in same bar, sc in back bar of next sc, turn. *(2 sc)*

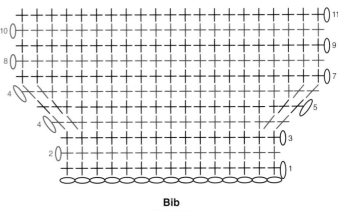

Back Bar of Single Crochet

Rows 2–20: Ch 1, sc in each sc across, turn.

Row 21: Ch 6, sk first sc, sl st in last sc. Fasten off.

Button Strap

Row 1: Join passionfruit in back bar of sc on rnd 1 of Top Trim below marker on opposite side from Buttonhole Strap, ch 1, sc in same bar, sc in back bar of next sc, turn. *(2 sc)*

Rows 2–26: Ch 1, sc in each sc across, turn.

At end of last row, fasten off.

With sewing needle and matching thread, sew buttons on end of Button Strap. ●

Bib
Base Stitch Diagram

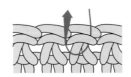

Bib
Cherry Stitch Diagram

STITCH KEY

◯ Chain (ch)

• Slip stitch (sl st)

+ Single crochet (sc)

⊤ Double crochet (dc)

⋏ or ⋀ Single crochet decrease (sc dec)

⋏⋏ Shell

✳ Marker

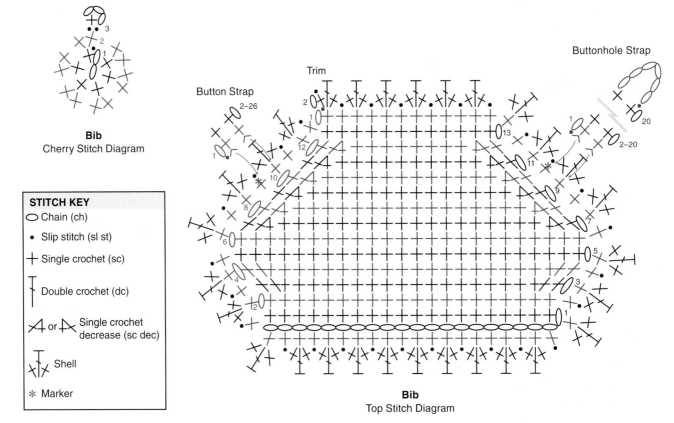

Button Strap

Trim

Buttonhole Strap

Bib
Top Stitch Diagram

Sweater

Skill Level
 ■■□□ EASY

Finished Size
Newborn

Finished Measurements
Chest: 15 inches in circumference

Sleeve: 4½ inches long

Materials

- Sirdar Snuggly Crofter DK light (DK) weight nylon/acrylic yarn (1¾ oz/179 yds/50g per skein):
  1 skein #182 Annabelle
- Size D/3/3.25mm crochet hook or size needed to obtain gauge
- Tapestry needle

Gauge
18 hdc = 4 inches; 16 rows = 4 inches

Pattern Notes
Sweater is worked in 1 piece from front to back then seamed 1 each side from wrist to hem.

Chain-2 at beginning of row does not count as stitch unless otherwise stated.

Join with slip stitch as indicated unless otherwise stated.

Sweater
Row 1 (RS): Ch 34, hdc in 3rd ch from hook and in each rem ch across, turn. *(32 hdc)*

Rows 2–17: Ch 2 *(see Pattern Notes)*, hdc in each hdc across, turn. Fasten off.

Row 18: Ch 20, with WS facing, **join** *(see Pattern Notes)* in first st, ch 2, hdc in same st, hdc in each rem st across, ch 22, turn. *(42 chs, 32 hdc)*

Row 19: Hdc in 3rd ch from hook and in each rem ch and hdc across, turn. *(72 hdc)*

Rows 20–24: Ch 2, hdc in each st across, turn.

Row 25: Ch 2, hdc in each of first 26 hdc, sl st in each of next 20 hdc, hdc in each rem hdc across, turn. *(52 hdc, 20 sl sts)*

Row 26: Ch 2, hdc in each of first 22 hdc, dc in each of next 4 hdc, ch 22, sk next 20 sl sts *(neck opening made)*, dc in each of next 4 hdc, hdc in each rem hdc across, turn. *(44 hdc, 8 dc, 20 chs)*

Row 27: Ch 2, hdc in each of first 26 sts, 22 hdc in next ch-20 sp, hdc in each rem st across, turn. *(74 hdc)*

Rows 28–34: Ch 2, hdc in each hdc across, turn. At end of last row, fasten off.

Row 35: With RS facing, sk first 20 hdc, join next st, ch 2, sc in each of next 34 hdc, turn, leaving rem sts unworked. *(34 sc)*

Rows 36–51: Ch 2, hdc in each st across, turn. At end of last row, fasten off.

Finishing
Fold work in half with neck opening at top. Sew sleeve and side seams. ●

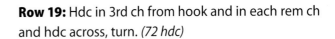

Car Seat Blanket

Skill Level

 ■■□□ EASY

Finished Measurements

17 inches wide x 25 inches long

Materials

- Berroco Weekend DK light (DK) weight acrylic/cotton yarn (3½ oz/268 yds/100g per hank):
    1 hank each #2925 taffy,
      #2902 vanilla and #2910 cornsilk
- Size F/5/3.75mm crochet hook or size needed to obtain gauge
- Tapestry needle

Gauge

1 pattern rep = 2 inches; 11 pattern rows = 4 inches

Pattern Notes

Refer to Stitch Diagram as needed.

Chain-3 at beginning of row counts as first double crochet unless otherwise stated.

Join with slip stitch as indicated unless otherwise stated.

Special Stitch

Shell: 3 dc as indicated in instructions.

Blanket

Row 1: With taffy, ch 73, sc in 2nd ch from hook, sc in next ch, *ch 1, sk next 3 chs, **shell** (see Special Stitch) in each of next 2 chs, ch 1, sk next 3 chs, sc in each of next 2 chs, rep from * across, turn. *(14 shells)*

Row 2: Ch 3 (see Pattern Notes), dc in next sc, *ch 3, sk next 2 dc, sc in each of next 2 dc, ch 3, sk next 2 dc, dc in each of next 2 dc, rep from * across, **changing color** (see Stitch Guide) to cornsilk in last st, turn. Fasten off taffy.

Row 3: With cornsilk, ch 3, dc in next dc, *ch 1, sk next ch-3 sp, shell in each of next 2 sc, ch 1, sk next ch-3 sp, dc in each of next 2 dc, rep from * across, turn.

Row 4: Ch 3, dc in next dc, *ch 3, sk next 2 dc, sc in each of next 2 dc, ch 3, sk next 2 dc, dc in each of next 2 dc, rep from * across, changing color to vanilla in last st, turn. Fasten off cornsilk.

Row 5: With vanilla, rep row 3.

Row 6: Rep row 4, changing color to taffy in last st. Fasten off vanilla.

Row 7: With taffy, rep row 3.

Row 8: Rep row 4, changing color to vanilla in last st. Fasten off taffy.

Rows 9–62: [Rep rows 3–8 consecutively] 9 times. At end of last row, fasten off.

Border

Rnd 1: Join (*see Pattern Notes*) taffy in top right corner, ch 3, dc in each dc and ch across row 62 to last st, (dc, ch 3, dc) in last dc, working in row ends along side of work, 2 dc in each row end across, working across opposite side of foundation ch, (dc, ch 3, dc) in first ch, dc in each rem ch across to last ch, (dc, ch 3, dc) in last ch, working in row ends along opposite side, 2 dc in each row end across, (dc, ch 3) in same st as beg ch-3, join in top of beg ch-3.

Rnds 2 & 3: Ch 3, dc in each dc around, working (dc, ch 3, dc) in each corner ch-3 sp, join in top of beg ch-3.

At end of last rnd, fasten off. ●

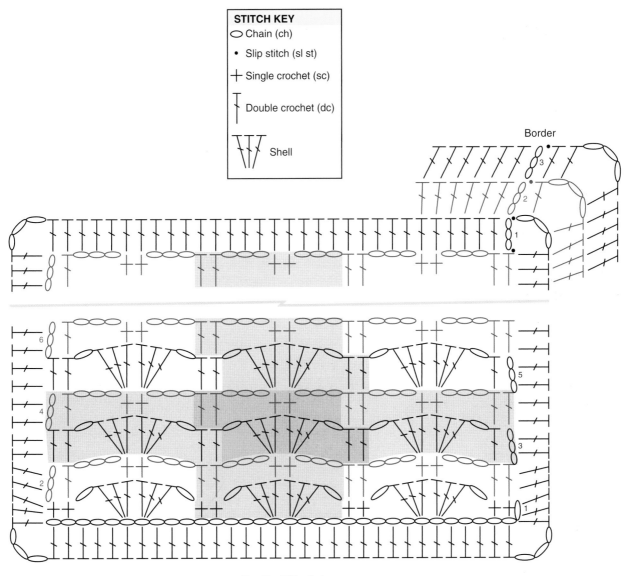

Car Seat Blanket
Reduced Sample of Stitch Diagram
Note: *Reps shown in gray.*

Bottle Cozy

Skill Level

 EASY

Finished Measurements

2¼ inches in diameter x 5 inches tall

Materials

- Premier Yarns Home Cotton medium (worsted) weight cotton/polyester yarn (2¾ oz/ 140 yds/80g per skein):
    1 skein #3804 yellow
- Size F/5/3.75mm crochet hook or size needed to obtain gauge
- Tapestry needle

Gauge

16 dc = 4 inches; 9 rows = 4 inches

Pattern Notes

Refer to Stitch Diagram as needed.

Cozy is worked in joined rounds with right side always facing; do not turn unless otherwise stated.

Join with slip stitch as indicated unless otherwise stated.

Chain-4 at beginning of round counts as first double crochet and chain-1 unless otherwise stated.

Cozy

Rnd 1 (RS): Ch 2, 6 sc in first ch, **join** *(see Pattern Notes)* in first sc. *(6 sc)*

Rnd 2: Ch 1, 2 sc in each sc around, join in first sc. *(12 sc)*

Rnd 3: Ch 1, sc in first sc, 2 sc in next sc, [sc in next sc, 2 sc in next sc] 5 times, join in first sc. *(18 sc)*

Rnd 4: Ch 1, sc in each of first 2 sc, 2 sc in next sc, [sc in each of next 2 sc, 2 sc in next sc] 5 times, join in first sc. *(24 sc)*

Rnd 5: Ch 1, sc in each of first 3 sc, 2 sc in next sc, [sc in each of next 3 sc, 2 sc in next sc] 5 times, join in first sc. *(30 sts)*

Rnd 6: Ch 1, sc in **back lp** *(see Stitch Guide)* of each sc around, join in first sc.

Rnd 7: Ch 1, sc in each sc around, join in first sc.

Rnd 8: Ch 4 *(see Pattern Notes)*, sk next sc, [dc in next sc, ch 1, sk next sc] 14 times, join in 3rd ch of beg ch-4. *(15 dc, 15 ch-1 sps)*

Rnds 9–14: Ch 4, [dc in next dc, ch 1] 14 times, join in 3rd ch of beg ch-4.

Rnd 15: Ch 1, sc in each dc and ch-1 sp around, join in first sc. *(30 sc)*

Rnd 16: Ch 1, sc in each sc around, join in first sc.

Rnd 17: Ch 1, sc in each of first 3 sc, **sc dec** *(see Stitch Guide)* in next 2 sc, [sc in each of next 3 sc, sc dec in next 2 sc] 5 times, join in first sc. *(24 sts)*

Fasten off. ●

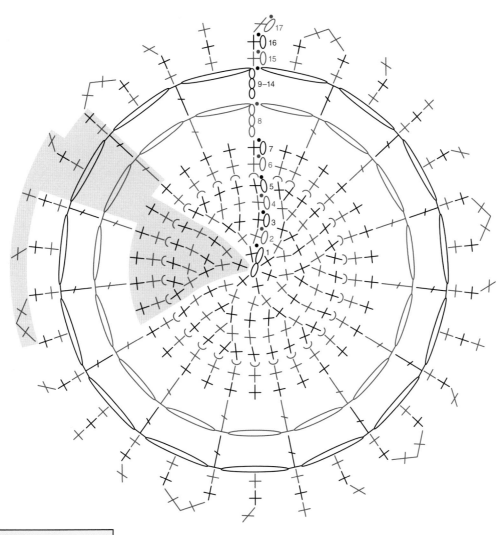

Bottle Cozy
Stitch Diagram
Note: Reps shown in gray.

STITCH KEY
◯ Chain (ch)

• Slip stitch (sl st)

✛ Single crochet (sc)

✝ Double crochet (dc)

⋏ Single crochet
  decrease (sc dec)

⌒ Work in back lp only

Cocoon

Skill Level

 ■■■□ INTERMEDIATE

Finished Measurements

18 inches in diameter x 13½ inches long

Materials

- Plymouth Yarn Cleo light (DK) weight cotton yarn (1¾ oz/ 125 yds/50g per hank):
    2 hanks #0162 powder sky
    1 hank #0163 regatta
- Size F/5/3.75mm crochet hook or size needed to obtain gauge
- Tapestry needle
- ½-inch-wide blue organza ribbon: 36 inches

Gauge

Rnds 1–5 = 4¼ inches in diameter; 9 pattern rows = 3 inches

Pattern Notes

Refer to Stitch Diagram as needed.

Cocoon is worked in joined rounds with right side always facing; do not turn unless otherwise stated.

Join with slip stitch as indicated unless otherwise stated.

Chain-2 at beginning of round does not count as stitch unless otherwise stated.

When changing color, drop lp of old color until next needed; do not fasten off unless otherwise stated.

Chain-3 at beginning of round counts as first double crochet unless otherwise stated.

Cocoon

Rnd 1: With powder sky, ch 4 (*sk chs count as dc*), 10 dc in first ch, **join** (*see Pattern Notes*) in first dc. (*11 dc*)

Rnd 2: Ch 2 (*see Pattern Notes*), 2 dc in each dc around, join in first dc. (*22 dc*)

Rnd 3: Ch 2, dc in first dc, 2 dc in next dc, [dc in next dc, 2 dc in next dc] 10 times, join in first dc. (*33 dc*)

Rnd 4: Ch 2, dc in each of first 2 dc, 2 dc in next dc, [dc in each of next 2 dc, 2 dc in next dc] 10 times, join in first dc. (*44 dc*)

Rnd 5: Ch 2, dc in each of first 3 dc, 2 dc in next dc, [dc in each of next 3 dc, 2 dc in next dc] 10 times, join in first dc. (*55 dc*)

Rnd 6: Ch 2, dc in each of first 4 dc, 2 dc in next dc, [dc in each of next 4 dc, 2 dc in next dc] 10 times, join in first dc. (*66 dc*)

Rnd 7: Ch 2, dc in each of first 5 dc, 2 dc in next dc, [dc in each of next 5 dc, 2 dc in next dc] 10 times, join in first dc. (*77 dc*)

Rnd 8: Ch 2, dc in each of first 6 dc, 2 dc in next dc, [dc in each of next 6 dc, 2 dc in next dc] 10 times, **changing color** (*see Stitch Guide and Pattern Notes*) to regatta in last st, join in first dc. (*88 dc*)

Rnd 9: With regatta, ch 1, sc in first dc, sc in each of next 3 dc, [**sc dec** (*see Stitch Guide*) in next 2 dc] twice, sc in each of next 3 dc, [2 sc in each of next 2 dc, sc in each of next 3 dc, {sc dec in next 2 dc} twice, sc in each of next 3 dc] 6 times, 2 sc in each of next 2 dc, sc in each of last 3 dc, changing color to powder sky in last st, join in first sc. (*88 sts*)

Rnd 10: Ch 3 (*see Pattern Notes*), dc in each of next 3 sts, [**dc dec** (*see Stitch Guide*) in next 2 sts] twice, dc in each of next 3 sts, [2 dc in each of next 2 sts, dc in each of next 3 sts, {dc dec in next 2 sts} twice, dc in

each of next 3 sts] 6 times, 2 dc in each of next 2 sts, dc in each of last 3 sts, changing color to regatta in last st, join in top of beg ch-3.

Rnd 11: Ch 1, sc in first st, sc in each of next 3 sts, [sc dec in next 2 sts] twice, sc in each of next 3 sts, [2 sc in each of next 2 sts, sc in each of next 3 sts, {sc dec in next 2 sts} twice, sc in each of next 3 sts] 6 times, 2 sc in each of next 2 sts, sc in each of last 3 sts, changing color to powder sky in last st, join in first sc.

Rnds 12–37: [Rep rnds 10 and 11 alternately] 13 times. At end of last rnd, fasten off regatta.

Rnd 38: Rep rnd 10.

Rnd 39: Ch 1, sc in first st, hdc in each of next 2 sts, dc in each of next 4 sts, hdc in each of next 2 sts, [sc in each of next 4 sts, hdc in each of next 2 sts, dc in each of next 4 sts, hdc in each of next 2 sts] 6 times, sc in each rem st around, join in first sc.

Rnd 40: Ch 2, dc in each st around, join in first dc. Fasten off.

Finishing

Weave ribbon between sts on rnd 38 and tie in front of Cocoon as shown in photo. Trim ends of ribbon to desired length. ●

STITCH KEY

◯ Chain (ch)

• Slip stitch (sl st)

+ Single crochet (sc)

T Half double crochet (hdc)

Ŧ Double crochet (dc)

⋉ or ⋀ Single crochet decrease (sc dec)

⋀ Double crochet decrease (dc dec)

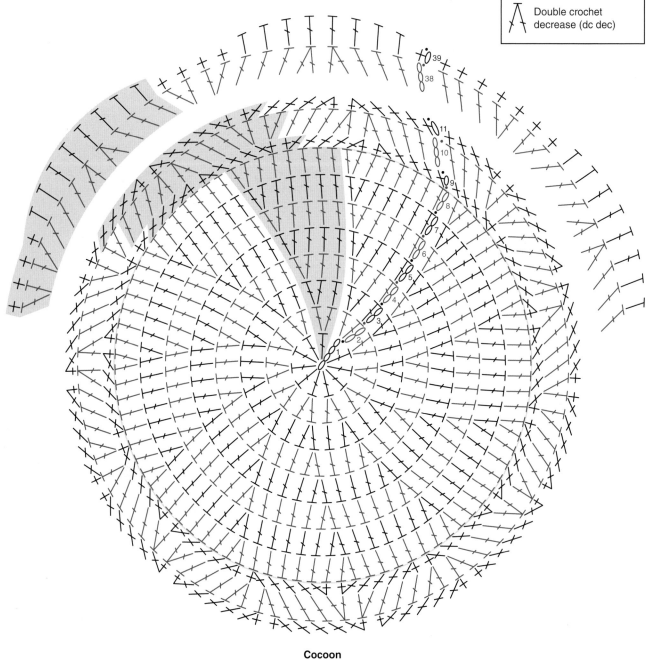

Cocoon
Stitch Diagram
Note: Reps shown in gray.

Traditional Baby Blanket

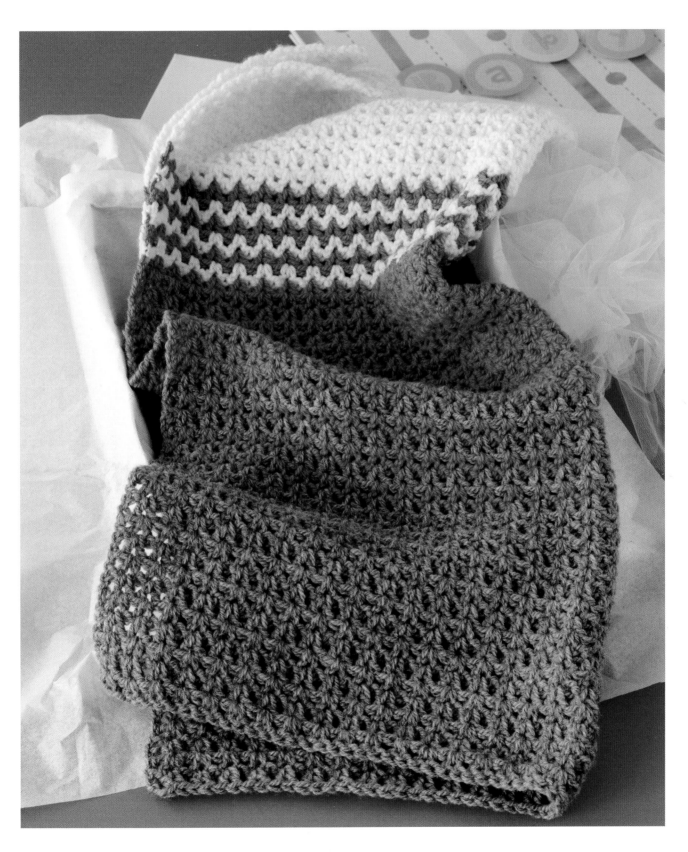

Skill Level

 **EASY**

Finished Measurements

24 inches wide x 31 inches long

Materials

- Plymouth Yarn Encore Worsted medium (worsted) weight acrylic/wool yarn (3½ oz/200 yds/100g per skein):
  2 skeins each #0256 ecru, #4045 serenity blue and #0194 medium grey
- Size H/8/5mm crochet hook or size needed to obtain gauge
- Tapestry needle

Gauge

13 sts = 4 inches; 9 rows = 4 inches

Pattern Notes

Refer to Stitch Diagram as needed.

Chain-3 at beginning of row counts as first double crochet unless otherwise stated.

Blanket

Row 1: With ecru, ch 73, 2 dc in 4th ch from hook *(sk chs count as dc)*, *sk next ch, 2 dc in next ch, rep from * across to last ch, dc in last ch, turn. *(72 sts)*

Row 2: Ch 3 *(see Pattern Notes)*, [2 dc in sp between next 2 dc] across to last st, dc in last st, turn.

Rows 3–17: [Rep row 2] 15 times.

Row 18: Ch 3, [2 dc in sp between next 2 dc] across to last st, dc in last st, **changing color** *(see Stitch Guide)* to blue in last st, turn. Fasten off ecru.

Row 19: With blue, ch 3, [2 dc in sp between next 2 dc] across to last st, dc in last st, changing color to ecru in last st, turn. Fasten off blue.

Rows 20–23: [Rep rows 18 and 19 alternately] twice.

Row 24: Rep row 18.

Rows 25–41: With blue, [rep row 2] 17 times.

Row 42: Ch 3, [2 dc in sp between next 2 dc] across to last st, dc in last st, changing color to grey in last st, turn. Fasten off blue.

Row 43: With grey, ch 3, [2 dc in sp between next 2 dc] across to last st, dc in last st, changing color to blue in last st, turn. Fasten off grey.

Rows 44–47: [Rep rows 42 and 43 alternately] twice.

Row 48: Rep row 42.

Rows 49–66: With grey, [rep row 2] 18 times. At end of last row, fasten off. ●

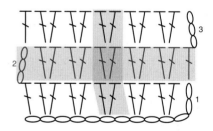

Traditional Baby Blanket
Reduced Sample of Stitch Diagram
***Note:** Reps shown in gray.*

STITCH KEY
◯ Chain (ch)
⊤ Double crochet (dc)

Jacket

Skill Level
 INTERMEDIATE

Finished Sizes
Instructions given to fit size 3 months; changes for 6 months and 12 months are in [ ].

Note: Size 12 months shown in photo.

Finished Measurements
Chest: 16 inches *(3 months)* [17 inches *(6 months)*, 18 inches *(12 months)*]

Length: 6 inches *(3 months)* [7 inches *(6 months)*, 7½ inches *(12 months)*]

Sleeve: 5¼ inches long *(3 months)* [6¼ inches *(6 months)*, 7¼ inches *(12 months)*]

Materials

- Cascade Yarns Cherub Aran medium (worsted) weight nylon/ acrylic yarn (3½ oz/240 yds/ 100g per skein):
    1 skein each #18 mocha, #05 baby mint and #09 ecru
- Size F/5/3.75mm crochet hook or size needed to obtain gauge
- Tapestry needle
- Sewing needle and matching thread
- ⅝-inch diameter button: 5
- Stitch markers: 4

Gauge
18 sc = 4 inches; 22 rows = 4 inches

Pattern Notes
Join with slip stitch as indicated unless otherwise stated.

Push buttons between double crochet stitches along row 3 of Trim on Left Front for buttonholes.

Chain-2 at beginning of row does not count as a stitch unless otherwise stated.

Sleeve is worked in continuous rounds; do not join or turn unless otherwise stated. Place marker in first stitch of round; move marker up as work progresses.

Jacket

Right Front
Row 1: With mocha, ch 19 [20, 21], sc in 2nd ch from hook and in each rem ch across, turn. *(18 [19, 20] sc)*

Rows 2 & 3 [2 & 3, 2–4]: Ch 1, sc in each sc across, turn. At end of last row, fasten off mocha.

Row 4 [4, 5]: With RS facing, **join** *(see Pattern Notes)* mint in first st, ch 1, sc in each sc across, turn.

Row 5 [5, 6]: Ch 1, sc in each sc across, turn. Fasten off mint.

In a Weekend: Baby Shower Gifts

Row 6 [6, 7]: With RS facing, join mocha in first st, ch 1, sc in each sc across, turn.

Rows 7 & 8 [7 & 8, 8–10]: Ch 1, sc in each sc across, turn. At end of last row, fasten off mocha.

Rows 9 & 10 [9 & 10, 11 & 12]: Rep rows 5 and 6. At end of last row, fasten off mint.

Rows 11–13 [11–13, 13–16]: Rep rows 7–10. At end of last row, fasten off mocha.

Row 14 [14, 17]: With RS facing, join cream in first st, ch 1, sc in each sc across, turn.

Rows 15–20 [15–26, 18–28]: Ch 1, sc in each sc across, turn.

Row 21 [27, 29]: Ch 1, sc in first sc, **sc dec** (see Stitch Guide) in next 2 sc, sc in each rem sc across, turn. (17 [18, 19] sts)

Row 22 [28, 30]: Ch 1, sc in each of first 14 [15, 16] sts, sc dec in next 2 sts, sc in last st, turn. (16 [17, 18] sts)

Row 23 [29, 31]: Rep row 21 [27, 29]. (15 [16, 17] sts)

Row 24 [30, 32]: Ch 1, sc in each of first 12 [13, 14] sts, sc dec in next 2 sts, sc in last st, turn. (14 [15, 16] sts)

Row 25 [31, 33]: Rep row 21 [27, 29]. (13 [14, 15] sts)

Row 26 [32, 34]: Ch 1, sc in each of first 10 [11, 12] sts, sc dec in next 2 sts, sc in last st, place marker in last st, turn. (12 [13, 14] sts)

Row 27 [33, 35]: Rep row 21 [27, 29]. (11 [12, 13] sts)

Row 28 [34, 36]: Ch 1, sc in each of first 8 [9, 10] sts, sc dec in next 2 sts, sc in last st, turn. (10 [11, 12] sts)

Row 29 [35, 37]: Rep row 21 [27, 29]. (9 [10, 11] sts)

Row 30 [36, 38]: Ch 1, sc in each of first 6 [7, 8] sts, sc dec in next 2 sts, sc in last st, turn. (8 [9, 10] sts)

Rows 31–33 [37–39, 39–41]: Ch 1, sc in each st across, turn.

At end of last row, fasten off.

Left Front

Rows 1–20 [1–26, 1–28]: Rep rows 1–20 [1–26, 1–28] of Right Front.

Row 21 [27, 29]: Ch 1, sc in each of first 15 [16, 17] sc, sc dec in next 2 sc, sc in last sc, turn. (17 [18, 19] sts)

Row 22 [28, 30]: Ch 1, sc in first st, sc dec in next 2 sts, sc in each rem st across, turn. (16 [17, 18] sts)

Row 23 [29, 31]: Ch 1, sc in each of first 13 [14, 15] sts, sc dec in next 2 sts, sc in last st, turn. (15 [16, 17] sts)

Row 24 [30, 32]: Rep row 22 [28, 30]. (14 [15, 16] sts)

Row 25 [31, 33]: Ch 1, sc in each of first 11 [12, 13] sts, sc dec in next 2 sts, sc in last st, turn. (13 [14, 15] sts)

Row 26 [32, 34]: Rep row 22 [28, 30]. Place marker in first st. (12 [13, 14] sts)

Row 27 [33, 35]: Ch 1, sc in each of first 9 [10, 11] sts, sc dec in next 2 sts, sc in last st, turn. (11 [12, 13] sts)

Row 28 [34, 36]: Rep row 22 [28, 30]. (10 [11, 12] sts)

Row 29 [35, 37]: Ch 1, sc in each of next 7 [8, 9] sts, sc dec in next 2 sts, sc in last st, turn. (9 [10, 11] sts)

Row 30 [36, 38]: Rep row 22 [28, 30]. (8 [9, 10] sts)

Rows 31–33 [37–39, 39–41]: Ch 1, sc in each st across, turn.

At end of last row, fasten off.

Back Panel

Row 1: With mocha, ch 37 [39, 42], sc in 2nd ch from hook and in each rem ch across, turn. (36 [38, 41] sts)

Rows 2–13 [2–13, 2–16]: Rep rows 2–13 [2–13, 2–16] of Right Front.

Rows 14–33 [14–39, 17–41]: Ch 1, sc in each st across, turn. Place marker in first and last st on row 17 [19, 21].

With RS tog, sew shoulder seams. Sew side seams from bottom up to markers on row 17 [21, 21] of Back. Turn garment RS out.

Hood

Row 1: Join cream in marked st on row 26 [32, 34] of Left Front, ch 1, evenly sp 34 [36, 40] sc across Left Front neckline, along Back and across Right Front neckline to next marker, turn. *(34 [36, 40] sts)*

Rows 2–19 [2–22, 2–23]: Ch 1, sc in each sc across, turn.

Row 20 [23, 24]: Ch 1, sc in each of first 12 [13, 15] sc, [sc dec in next 2 sts] 5 times, sc in each rem st across, turn. *(29 [31, 35] sts)*

Row 28: Ch 1, sc in each of first 10 [11, 13] sts, [sc dec in next 2 sts] 2 times, sc in next st, [sc dec in next 2 sts] 2 times, sc in each rem st across, turn. *(25 [27, 31] sts)*

Leaving long end for sewing, fasten off.

Sew top seam of Hood.

Trim

Row 1: Join mocha in first row end on Left Front, working in row ends along Fronts and Hood, sc in each row end around to last row end on Right Front. Fasten off.

Row 2: Join mint in first st on row 1, ch 1, sc in each st across. Fasten off.

Row 3: Join mocha in first st on row 2, **ch 2** *(see Pattern Notes)*, dc in each st across. Fasten off.

With sewing needle and thread, sew buttons evenly sp along row 3 of Trim on Right Front as shown in photo.

Sleeve

Rnd 1: Join cream in first row end under arm, working in row ends, 36 [42, 48] sc evenly sp around opening, **do not join** *(see Pattern Notes)*. **Place marker** in first st *(see Pattern Notes)*. *(36 [42, 48] sts)*

Rnd[s] 2 [2–4, 2–6]: Sc in next st and in each rem st around.

Rnd 3 [5, 7]: [Sc in each of next 4 sts, sc dec in next 2 sts] 6 times. *(30 [36, 42] sts)*

Rnd 4 [6, 8]: [Sc in each of next 3 sts, sc dec in next 2 sts] 6 times. *(24 [30, 36] sts)*

Rnds 5–19 [7–24, 9–28]: Sc in next st and in each rem st around. Fasten off cream.

Rnd 20 [25, 29]: Join mocha in first st, ch 1, sc in same st and in each rem st around.

Rnds 21 & 22 [26 & 27, 30–32]: Sc in next st and in each rem st around. At end of last rnd, fasten off mocha.

Rnd 23 [28, 33]: Join mint in first st, ch 1, sc in same st and in each rem st around.

Rnd 24 [29, 34]: Sc in next st and in each rem st around. Fasten off mint.

Rnd 25 [30, 35]: Rep rnd 20 [25, 29].

Fasten off.

Rep for 2nd Sleeve. ●

Car Seat Carrier Cover

Skill Level

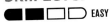 EASY

Finished Measurements

24 inches wide x 40 inches long

Materials

- Plymouth Yarn Encore Worsted Colorspun medium (worsted) weight acrylic/wool yarn (3½ oz/ 200 yds/100g per skein):
  - 3 skeins #7651 brights
- Plymouth Yarn Encore Worsted medium (worsted) weight acrylic/wool yarn (3½ oz/ 200 yds/100g per skein):
  - 1 skein #0194 medium grey
- Size H/8/5mm crochet hook or size needed to obtain gauge
- Tapestry needle
- 1½-inch button: 2
- Sewing needle and matching thread
- Stitch markers: 4

Gauge

1 pattern rep = 3½ inches; 7 pattern rows = 4 inches

Pattern Notes

Refer to Stitch Diagram as needed.

Chain-3 at beginning of row counts as first double crochet unless otherwise stated.

Join with slip stitch as indicated unless otherwise stated.

Special Stitch

Shell: 3 dc as indicated in instructions.

Cover

Row 1: With brights, ch 91, dc in 4th ch from hook *(sk chs count as first dc)*, dc in each of next 3 chs, *ch 3, **shell** *(see Special Stitch)* in next ch, sk next 3 chs, sc in next ch, ch 3, sk next 2 chs, dc in each of next 5 chs, rep from * across, turn. *(40 dc, 14 ch-3 sps, 7 shells, 7 sc)*

Row 2: Ch 3 *(see Pattern Notes)*, dc in each of next 4 dc, *ch 3, shell in next ch-3 sp, sc in next ch-3 sp, ch 3, dc in each of next 5 dc, rep from * across, turn.

Rows 3–64: Rep row 2. Fasten off. Place marker in 3rd and 5th shells on rows 22 and 28.

Row 65: Join *(see Pattern Notes)* grey in first st, ch 3, dc in next dc and in each rem dc across, working 2 dc in each ch-3 sp, turn. *(89 dc)*

Rows 66–70: Ch 3, dc in next st and in each rem st across, turn. Fasten off.

Edging

Row 1: Working across opposite side of foundation ch, join grey in first ch, ch 3, dc in next ch and in each rem ch across, turn. *(89 dc)*

Rows 2–6: Ch 3, dc in next st and in each rem st across, turn. At end of last row, fasten off.

Strap
Make 2.

Row 1: With grey, ch 23, sc in 2nd ch from hook and in each rem ch across, turn. *(22 sc)*

Row 2: Ch 1, sc in each sc across, turn.

Row 3: Ch 1, sc in each of first 2 sc, ch 3, sk next 3 chs, sc in each rem sc across, turn. *(19 sc, 1 ch-3 sp)*

Rows 4 & 5: Ch 1, sc in each st across, working 3 sc in ch-3 sp, turn. At end of last row, fasten off. *(22 sc)*

With tapestry needle and grey, sew short end of 1 Strap securely across first marked shell on row 22. Rep with 2nd Strap on 2nd marked shell on row 22.

With sewing needle and matching thread, sew 1 button on each marked shell on row 28. ●

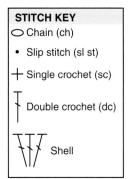

STITCH KEY

⬭ Chain (ch)

• Slip stitch (sl st)

+ Single crochet (sc)

⊤ Double crochet (dc)

⟎ Shell

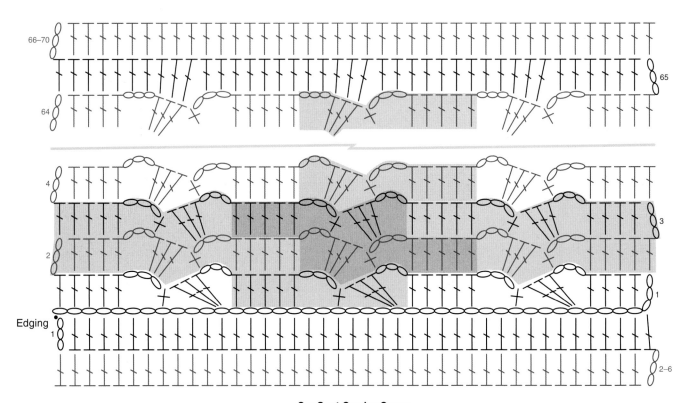

Car Seat Carrier Cover
Reduced Sample of Stitch Diagram
Note: Reps shown in gray.

STITCH GUIDE

STITCH ABBREVIATIONS

beg .... begin/begins/beginning
bpdc .... back post double crochet
bpsc .... back post single crochet
bptr .... back post treble crochet
CC .... contrasting color
ch(s) .... chain(s)
ch- .... refers to chain or space
      previously made (i.e., ch-1 space)
ch sp(s) .... chain space(s)
cl(s) .... cluster(s)
cm .... centimeter(s)
dc .... double crochet (singular/plural)
dc dec .... double crochet 2 or more
      stitches together, as indicated
dec .... decrease/decreases/decreasing
dtr .... double treble crochet
ext .... extended
fpdc .... front post double crochet
fpsc .... front post single crochet
fptr .... front post treble crochet
g .... gram(s)
hdc .... half double crochet
hdc dec .... half double crochet 2 or more
      stitches together, as indicated
inc .... increase/increases/increasing
lp(s) .... loop(s)
MC .... main color
mm .... millimeter(s)
oz .... ounce(s)
pc .... popcorn(s)
rem .... remain/remains/remaining
rep(s) .... repeat(s)
rnd(s) .... round(s)
RS .... right side
sc .... single crochet (singular/plural)
sc dec .... single crochet 2 or more
      stitches together, as indicated
sk .... skip/skipped/skipping
sl st(s) .... slip stitch(es)
sp(s) .... space(s)/spaced
st(s) .... stitch(es)
tog .... together
tr .... treble crochet
trtr ....triple treble
WS .... wrong side
yd(s) .... yard(s)
yo .... yarn over

YARN CONVERSION

OUNCES TO GRAMS		GRAMS TO OUNCES	
1	28.4	25	⅞
2	56.7	40	1⅔
3	85.0	50	1¾
4	113.4	100	3½

UNITED STATES		UNITED KINGDOM
sl st (slip stitch)	=	sc (single crochet)
sc (single crochet)	=	dc (double crochet)
hdc (half double crochet)	=	htr (half treble crochet)
dc (double crochet)	=	tr (treble crochet)
tr (treble crochet)	=	dtr (double treble crochet)
dtr (double treble crochet)	=	ttr (triple treble crochet)
skip	=	miss

Single crochet decrease (sc dec): (Insert hook, yo, draw lp through) in each of the sts indicated, yo, draw through all lps on hook.

Example of 2-sc dec

Half double crochet decrease (hdc dec): (Yo, insert hook, yo, draw lp through) in each of the sts indicated, yo, draw through all lps on hook.

Example of 2-hdc dec

Reverse single crochet (reverse sc): Ch 1, sk first st, working from left to right, insert hook in next st from front to back, draw up lp on hook, yo and draw through both lps on hook.

Chain (ch): Yo, pull through lp on hook.

Single crochet (sc): Insert hook in st, yo, pull through st, yo, pull through both lps on hook.

Double crochet (dc): Yo, insert hook in st, yo, pull through st, [yo, pull through 2 lps] twice.

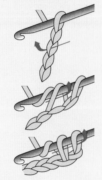

Double crochet decrease (dc dec): (Yo, insert hook, yo, draw lp through, yo, draw through 2 lps on hook) in each of the sts indicated, yo, draw through all lps on hook.

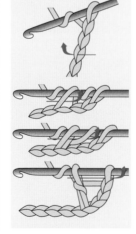

Example of 2-dc dec

Front loop (front lp) Back loop (back lp)

Front Loop   Back Loop

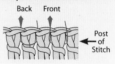

Front post stitch (fp): Back post stitch (bp): When working post st, insert hook from right to left around post of st on previous row.

Back   Front

Post of Stitch

Half double crochet (hdc): Yo, insert hook in st, yo, pull through st, yo, pull through all 3 lps on hook.

Double treble crochet (dtr): Yo 3 times, insert hook in st, yo, pull through st, [yo, pull through 2 lps] 4 times.

Treble crochet decrease (tr dec): Holding back last lp of each st, tr in each of the sts indicated, yo, pull through all lps on hook.

Example of 2-tr dec

Slip stitch (sl st): Insert hook in st, pull through both lps on hook.

Chain color change (ch color change) Yo with new color, draw through last lp on hook.

Double crochet color change (dc color change) Drop first color, yo with new color, draw through last 2 lps of st.

Treble crochet (tr): Yo twice, insert hook in st, yo, pull through st, [yo, pull through 2 lps] 3 times.